BRAIN GAMES

Get Ready for
KINDERGARTEN

Picture Puzzles
for Growing Minds

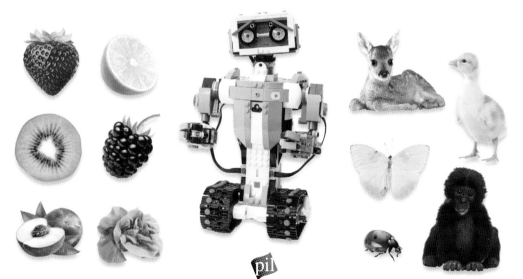

pil

Publications International, Ltd.

What is STEM?

The acronym STEM stands for Science, Technology, Engineering, and Math. STEM is not just about knowledge, but also about how to obtain, process, and apply that knowledge. The skills involved include observation, investigation, understanding, and problem-solving. Introducing these concepts early on can help foster children's curiosity and build the skills they need to understand the world around them.

Play to LEARN.

The picture puzzles in this book encourage children to explore and learn, even as they play! Sometimes puzzlers are encouraged to look closely at a picture for details, or to take a wider view to plan their path through a maze. At other times, they can try out their logic skills to solve the puzzle. Throughout the book, bright, colorful pictures and challenging games keep children interested and entertained.

The puzzles may be done in any order, and with or without help from an adult. Kids can check the table of contents to find their favorite types of puzzles, or dive straight in!

Contents

Contents

Follow Me

Find the path that goes through every cat. But avoid the flower!

START

FINISH

6

Answers on page 105.

Find My Shadow

Can you circle the shadow that matches the strawberry?

Answers on page 105.

Hidden Pattern

Search for this pattern of pictures inside the big grid.

Answers on page 105.

Memory

Look at this picture for 1 minute. Remember as much as you can! Then turn the page.

What is different in this picture? Find 4 things that are different.

Answers on page 105.

Making Groups

Write the number of animals that fit in each group. Some might be in more than one group!

Can fly? _____

Is yellow? _____

Is a mammal? _____

Can breathe underwater? _____

What Is It?

These objects are all cut up! Can you see what each one is?

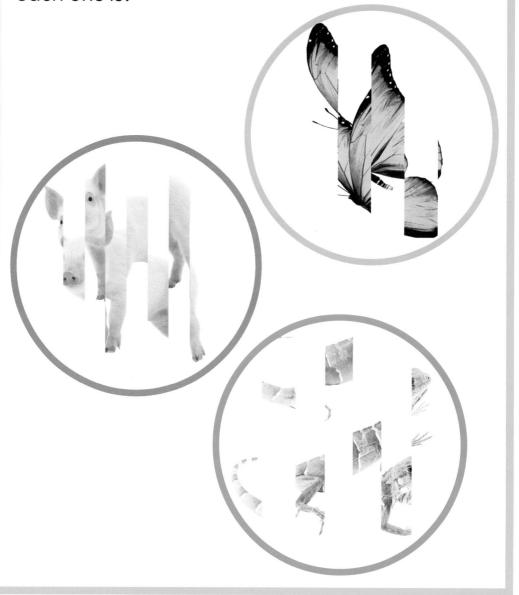

Answers on page 106.

Find It

Circle the objects in the photo that match each shadow.

Secret Code

One word below is in code. Each symbol in the code stands for one letter. Using the key, write each letter above the matching symbol. What is the coded word?

A _ _ _ _ can roar.

I = 🌼   L = 🍐   N = 🚗   O = 🐌

Answers on page 106.

Which One?

I lost my pet. Use the clues to figure out which pet is mine.

> My pet is yellow.
>
> My pet is an insect.
>
> My pet can fly.

Follow Me

Find the path that goes through every carrot. But avoid the corn!

START

FINISH

Answers on page 107.

Match It

Draw a line to connect each vehicle to the first letter of its name.

Hidden Pattern

Search for this pattern of pictures inside the big grid.

Answers on page 107.

Zoom In

Draw a line from each zoomed picture to the object it matches.

Answers on page 108.

Hide and Seek

Circle the **3** butterflies hiding in the forest.

Answers on page 108.

Two by Two

Draw a line to connect each food to its twin.

Answers on page 108.

Step by Step

Follow each step to get to school.

1	START	
2	GO ➡ 3 spots	
3	GO ⬇ 2 spots	
4	GO ⬅ 2 spots	

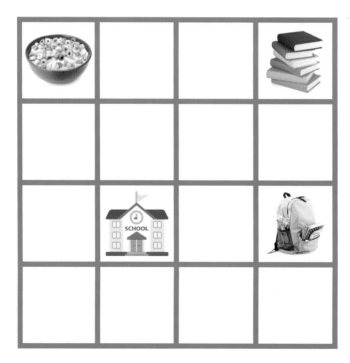

Answers on page 108.

Making Groups

Write the number of foods and drinks that fit in each group. Some might be in more than one group!

Is a fruit? _____

Is a vegetable? _____

Is baked? _____

Is a drink? _____

Missing Piece

Circle the piece that goes in the missing spot.

Answers on page 109.

Find It

Circle the objects in the photo that match each shadow.

Answers on page 109.

Two by Two

Draw a line to connect each flower to its twin.

Answers on page 109.

What Is It?

These objects are all cut up! Can you see what each one is?

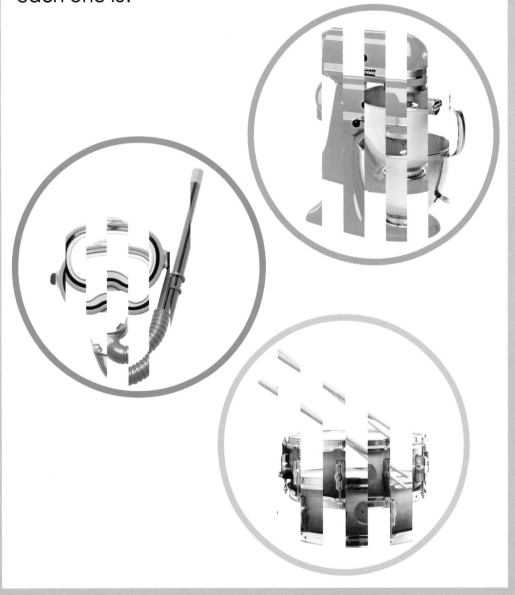

Follow Me

Decorate the fish tank! Find the path that goes through each fish and decoration, but avoid the cat!

Answers on page 110.

Do It

Shake this book! Then turn the page.

What happened?

Answers on page 110.

Find My Shadow

Can you circle the shadow that matches the pepper?

Draw It

The radish is missing its leaves. Can you draw what is missing?

Answers on page 111.

Secret Code

One word below is in code. Each symbol in the code stands for one letter. Using the key, write each letter above the matching symbol. What is the coded word?

Let's bake _ _ _ _ _ !

D = 🐔   A = ⛴️   B = 🍌   E = ◉   R = 🐟

Match It

Draw a line to connect each instrument to the first letter of its name.

Answers on page 111.

What Is Next?

Fill in the missing piece of each pattern.

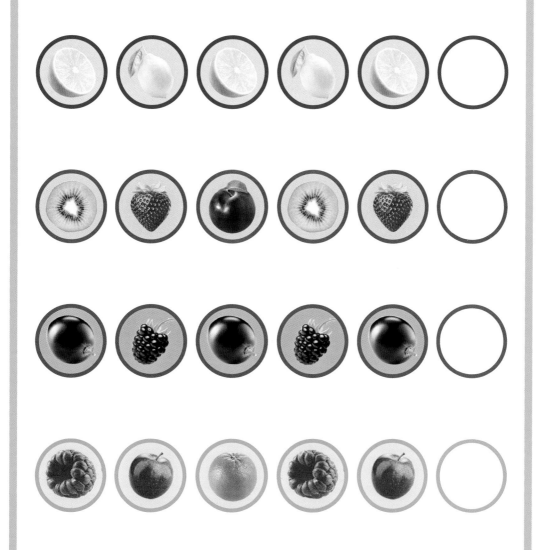

Hidden Pattern

Search for this pattern of pictures inside the big grid.

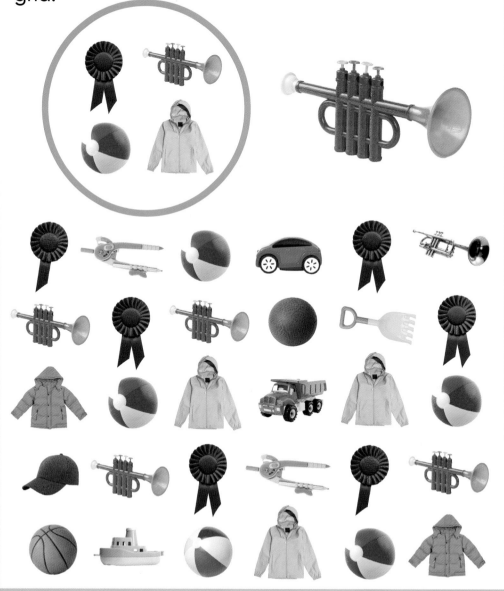

Answers on page 112.

Step by Step

Follow each step to build the robot.

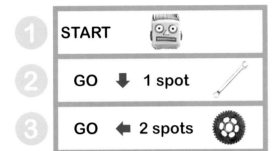

1. START

2. GO ↓ 1 spot

3. GO ← 2 spots

4. GO ↓ 2 spots

5. GO ← 2 spots

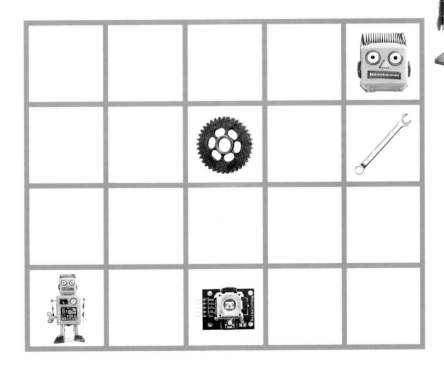

Zoom In

Draw a line from each zoomed picture to the object it matches.

Answers on page 112.

Memory

Look at this picture for 1 minute. Remember as much as you can! Then turn the page for step 2.

What is different in this picture? Find 5 things that are different.

Answers on page 112.

Missing Piece

Circle the piece that goes in the missing spot.

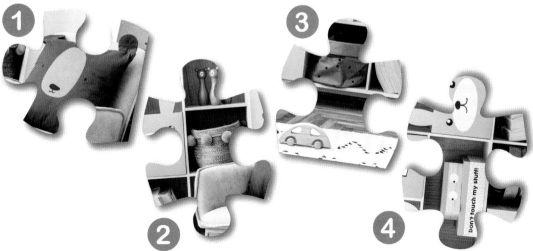

Find My Shadow

Can you circle the shadow the matches the zebra?

42

Answers on page 113.

Which One?

I lost something at the beach. Use the clues to figure out which object is mine.

My object is used in the water.

My object is something you wear.

My object is blue.

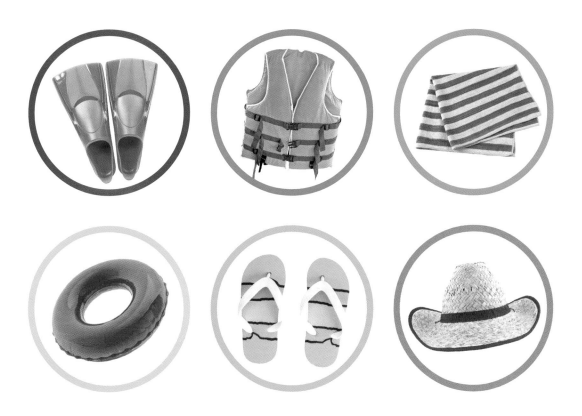

Hide and Seek

Circle the animals hiding in the ocean.

Answers on page 113.

Do It

Turn this book upside down! Then turn the page.

What happened?

Answers on page 114.

Making Groups

Write the number of vehicles that fit in each group.
Some might be in more than one group!

Can fly? _____

Has wheels? _____

Is red? _____

Is yellow? _____

Answers on page 114.

47

Find It

Circle the objects in the photo that match each shadow.

1   **2**   **3**   **4**

5

Answers on page 114.

Match It

Draw a line to connect each object to the first letter of its name.

Secret Code

One word below is in code. Each symbol in the code stands for one letter. Using the key, write each letter above the matching symbol. What is the coded word?

The _ _ _ _ _ _

makes music.

L = 🧢   O = 🐚   V = 🐭   N = 🧤   I = 🪇

50

Answers on page 115.

Draw It

The robot is missing a part. Can you draw what is missing?

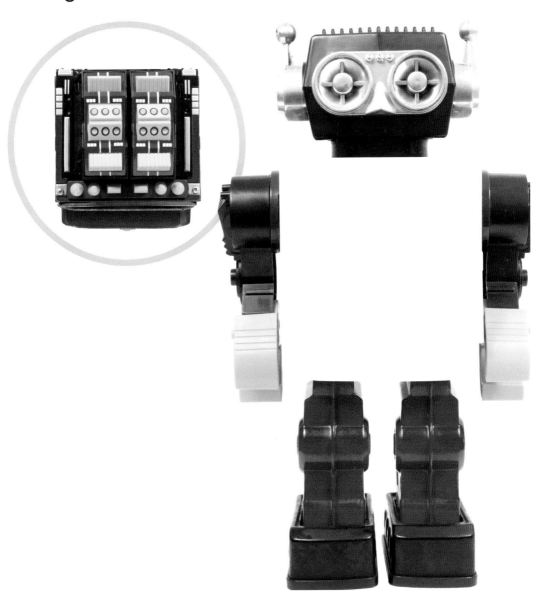

Follow Me

Find the path that goes through every dog. But avoid the flower!

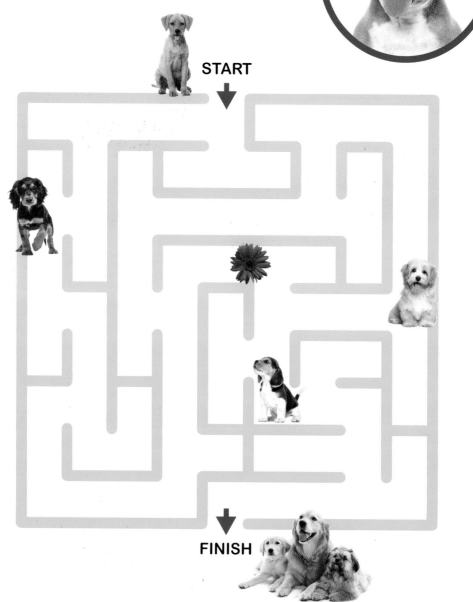

START

FINISH

52

Answers on page 115.

What Is Next?

Fill in the missing piece of each pattern.

Answers on page 115.

Hidden Pattern

Search for this pattern of pictures inside the big grid.

Answers on page 116.

What Is It?

These objects are all cut up! Can you see what each one is?

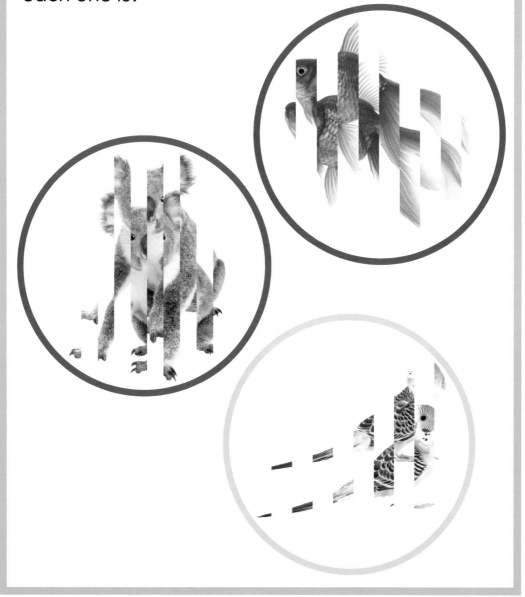

Missing Piece

Circle the piece that goes in the missing spot.

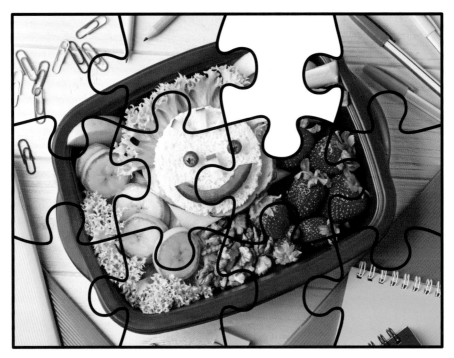

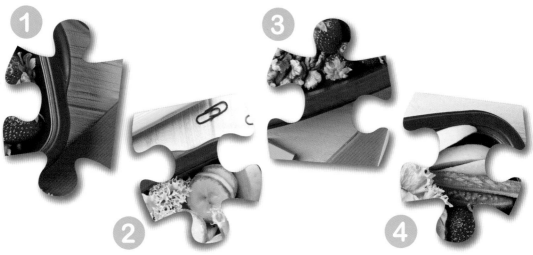

Answers on page 116.

Step by Step

Follow each step to make the salad.

1	START	
2	GO ➡ 5 spots	
3	GO ⬇ 3 spots	
4	GO ⬅ 4 spots	
5	GO ⬆ 2 spots	
6	GO ➡ 2 spots	

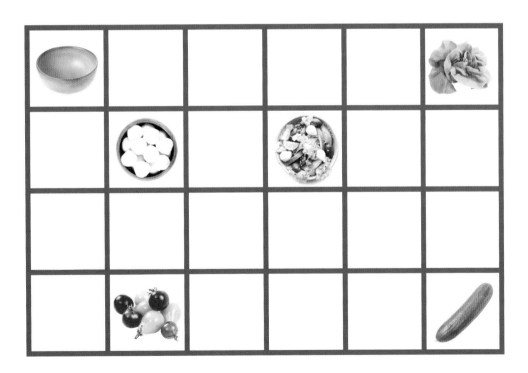

Zoom In

Draw a line from each zoomed picture to the object it matches.

Answers on page 117.

Out of Order

These pictures are out of order. Write 1, 2, 3, or 4 beside each picture to show the order they should go in.

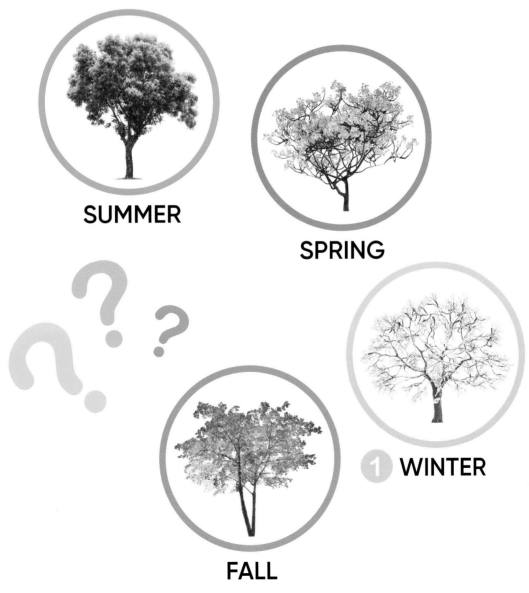

SUMMER

SPRING

WINTER

FALL

Find It

Circle the objects in the photo that match each shadow.

Answers on page 117.

What Changed?

Circle the **4** differences between the birds on the top and the birds on the bottom.

What Is Next?

Fill in the missing piece of each pattern.

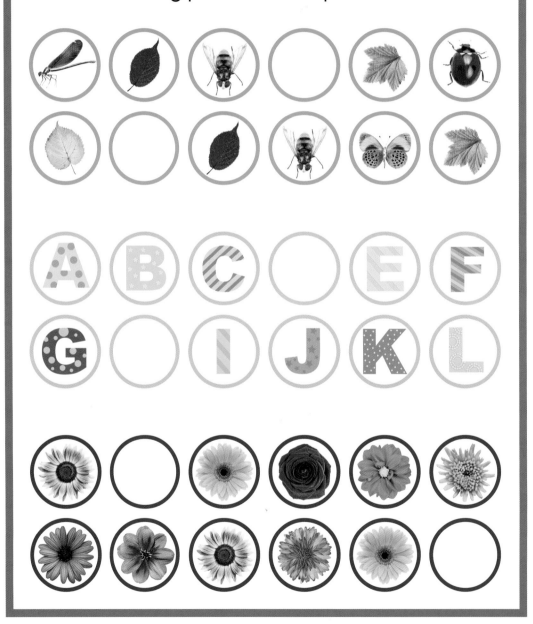

Answers on page 118.

Find My Shadow

Can you circle the shadow that matches the scissors?

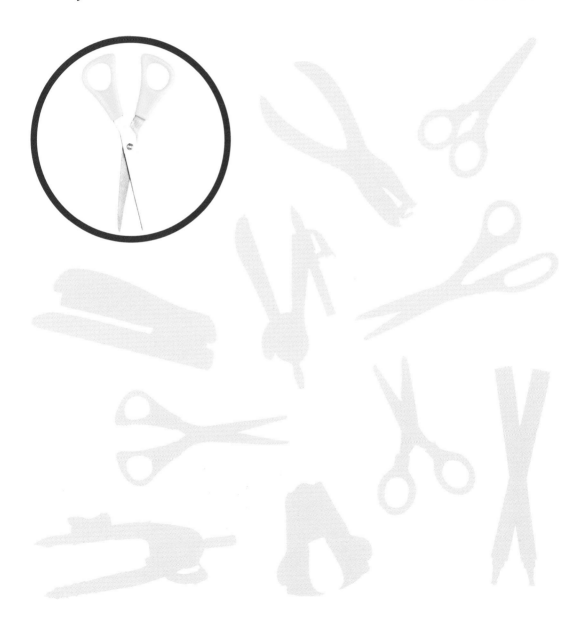

What Is It?

These objects are all cut up! Can you see what each one is?

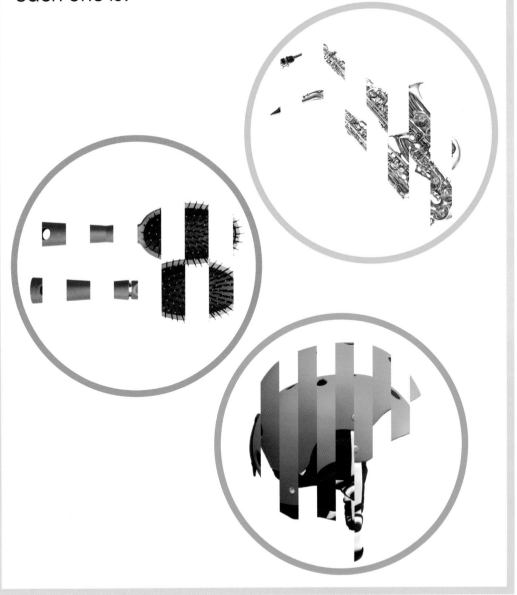

Answers on page 118.

What Changed?

Circle the 5 differences between the toys on the top and the toys on the bottom.

Two by Two

Draw a line to connect each fish to its twin.

Answers on page 119.

Do It

Pat this book! Then turn the page.

What happened?

Hide and Seek

Circle the fruits and veggies hiding in the garden.

Answers on page 119.

Which One?

I lost my fruit. Use the clues to figure out which fruit is mine.

My fruit does not have a pit.

My fruit does not have any pink on it.

My fruit does not have a stem.

Answers on page 119.

Match It

Draw a line to connect each animal to the first letter of its name.

Secret Code

One word below is in code. Each symbol in the code stands for one letter. Using the key, write each letter above the matching symbol. What is the coded word?

The _ _ _ _ _ _ _

goes fast.

C =  L = E = I = Y =   B =

Answers on page 120.

Hidden Pattern

Search for this pattern of pictures inside the big grid.

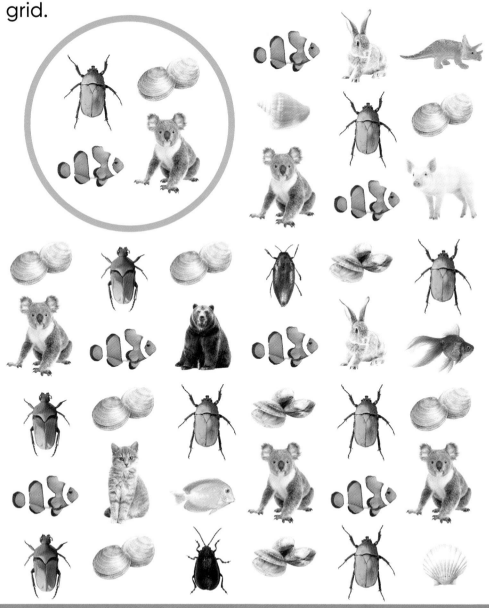

Making Groups

Write the numbers of the sea creatures that fit in each group. Some might be in more than one group!

Is blue? _____

Can swim? _____

Is not a mammal? _____

Answers on page 120.

Missing Piece

Circle the piece that goes in the missing spot.

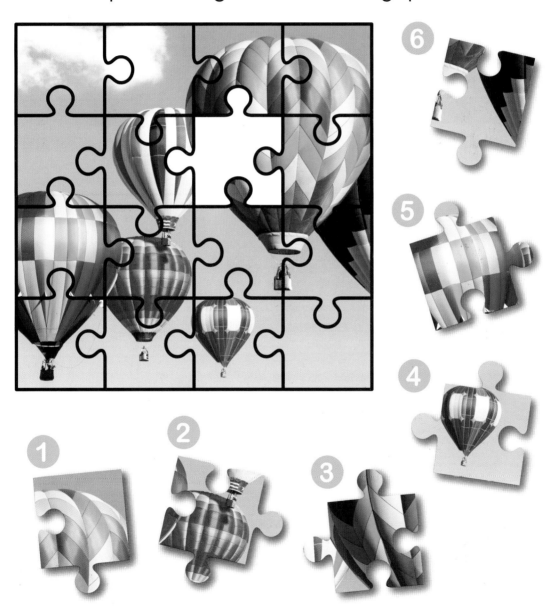

Two by Two

Draw a line to connect each butterfly to its twin.

Answers on page 121.

Zoom In

Draw a line from each zoomed picture to the object it matches.

Draw It

The butterfly is missing some parts. Can you draw what is missing?

Answers on page 121.

What Is Next?

Fill in the missing piece of each pattern.

Follow Me

Find the path that goes through every grocery item. But avoid the hungry bunny!

START

FINISH

Answers on page 122.

Find My Shadow

Circle the shadow that matches the bug.

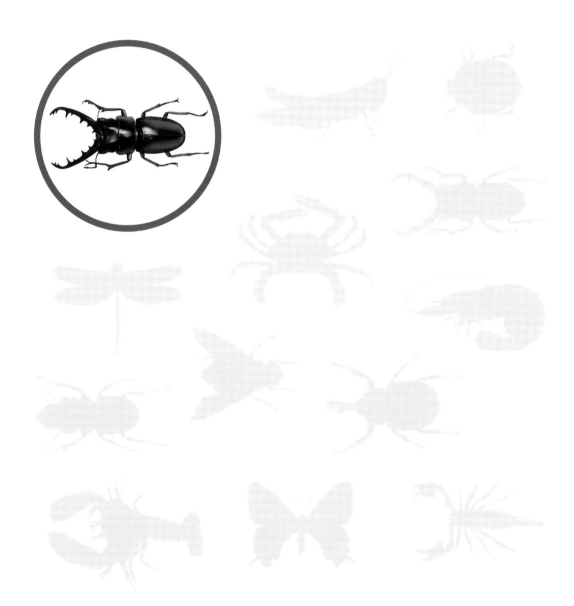

Out of Order

These pictures are out of order. Write 1, 2, 3, or 4 beside each picture to show the order they should go in.

Answers on page 122.

Step by Step

Follow each step to build the birdhouse.

① START

② GO ← 2 spots

③ GO ↓ 2 spots

④ GO ➡ 5 spots

⑤ GO ↑ 3 spots

⑥ GO ← 2 spots

⑦ GO ↓ 2 spots

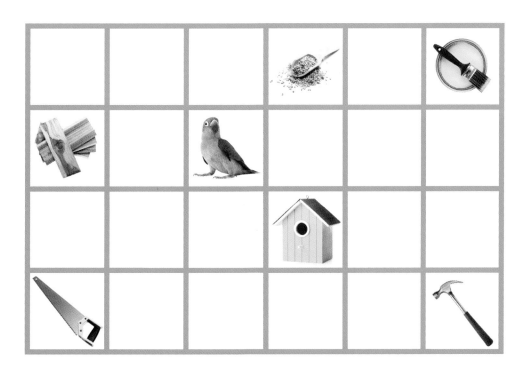

Secret Code

One word below is in code. Each symbol in the code stands for one letter. Using the key, write each letter above the matching symbol. What is the coded word?

The _ _ _ _ _ _ _ _

is big.

P =   N =   H =   T =   L =   E =   A =

Answers on page 123.

Which One?

I lost my ball! Use the clues to figure out which ball is mine.

My ball is shaped like a sphere.

My ball has white on it.

My ball is kicked, not thrown.

Hidden Pattern

Search for this pattern of pictures inside the big grid.

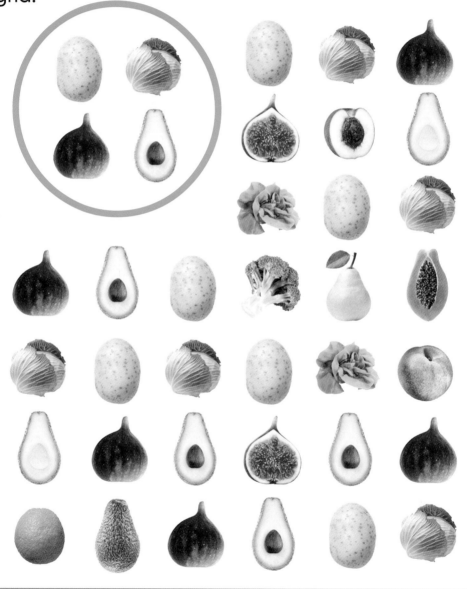

Answers on page 123.

Memory

Look at this picture for 1 minute. Remember as much as you can! Then turn the page for step 2.

What is different in this picture? Find 5 things that are different.

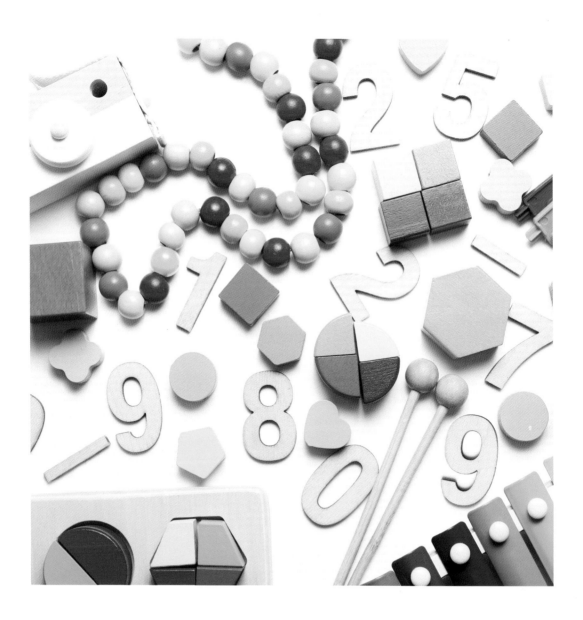

Answers on page 124.

Secret Code

One word below is in code. Each symbol in the code stands for one letter. Using the key, write each letter above the matching symbol. What is the coded word?

The _ _ _ _ _ _ _ _

is rainbow.

B = 🎖 L = 🐦 E = 🍋 U = ⭐ A = 🎺 R = 🧥 M = 🐋

Hide and Seek

Circle the animals hiding in the forest

1  **2** **3** **4**

Answers on page 124.

Two by Two

Draw a line to match each leaf to its twin.

Match It

Draw a line to connect each sea animal to the first letter of its name.

Answers on page 125.

Step by Step

Follow each step to fill the flower basket.

1	START
2	GO ➡ 1 spot
3	GO ⬆ 2 spots
4	GO ⬅ 2 spots

5	GO ⬆ 1 spot
6	GO ⬅ 3 spots
7	GO ⬇ 2 spots
8	GO ➡ 2 spots

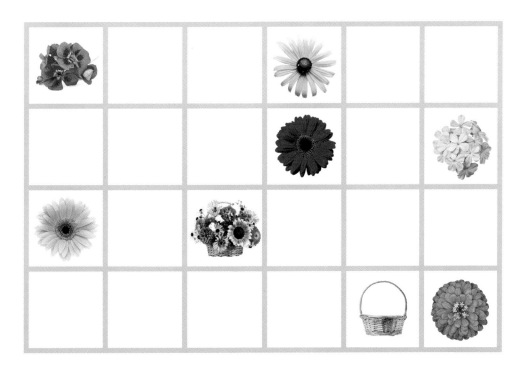

Answers on page 125.

93

Draw It

The vase is missing its flowers. Can you draw what is missing?

Answers on page 125.

Out of Order

These pictures are out of order. Write 1, 2, 3, 4, or 5 beside each picture to show the order they should go in.

What Changed?

Circle the 5 differences between the instruments on the top and the instruments on the bottom.

Answers on page 126.

Hide and Seek

Circle the animals hiding in the snow.

1   2   3   4

Follow Me

Pack the suitcase! Find the path that goes through every item of clothing.

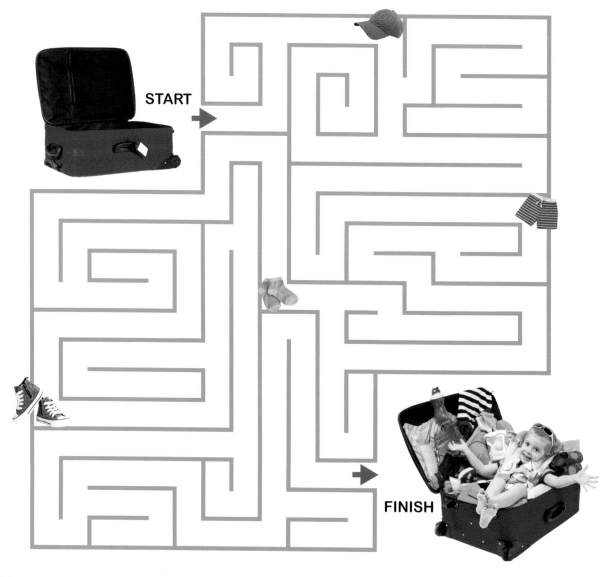

START

FINISH

98

Out of Order

These pictures are out of order. Write 1, 2, 3, 4, 5, or 6 beside each picture to show the order they should go in.

What Changed?

Circle the 5 differences between the clothes on the top and the clothes on the bottom.

Answers on page 127.

Find It

Circle the objects in the photo that match each shadow.

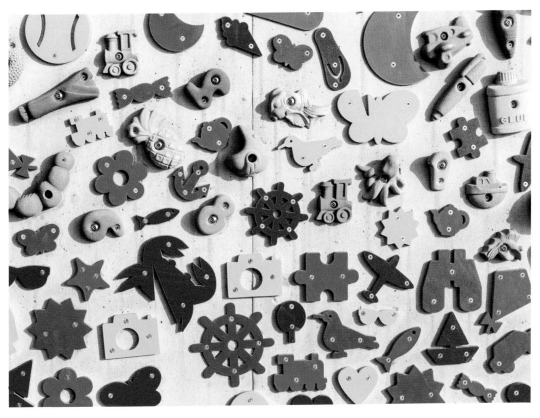

Missing Piece

Circle the piece that goes in the missing spot.

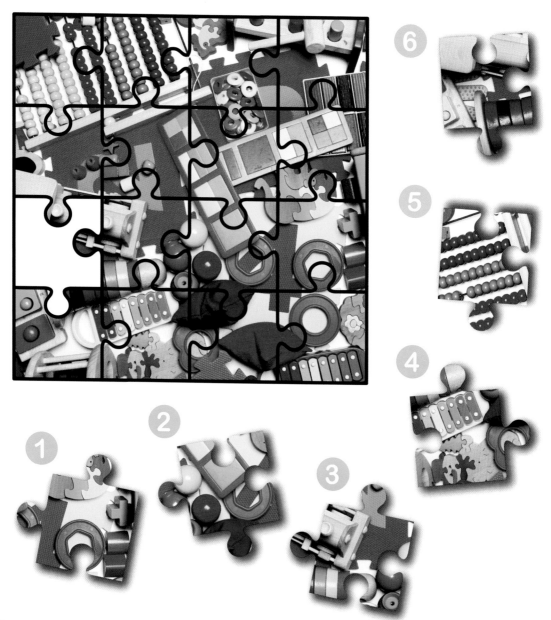

Answers on page 127.

Out of Order

These colors are out of order. Color the rainbow in the correct order!

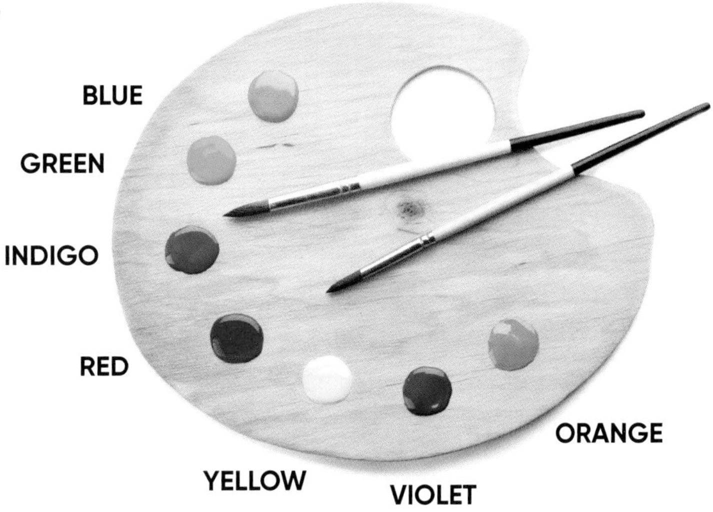

BLUE

GREEN

INDIGO

RED

YELLOW

VIOLET

ORANGE

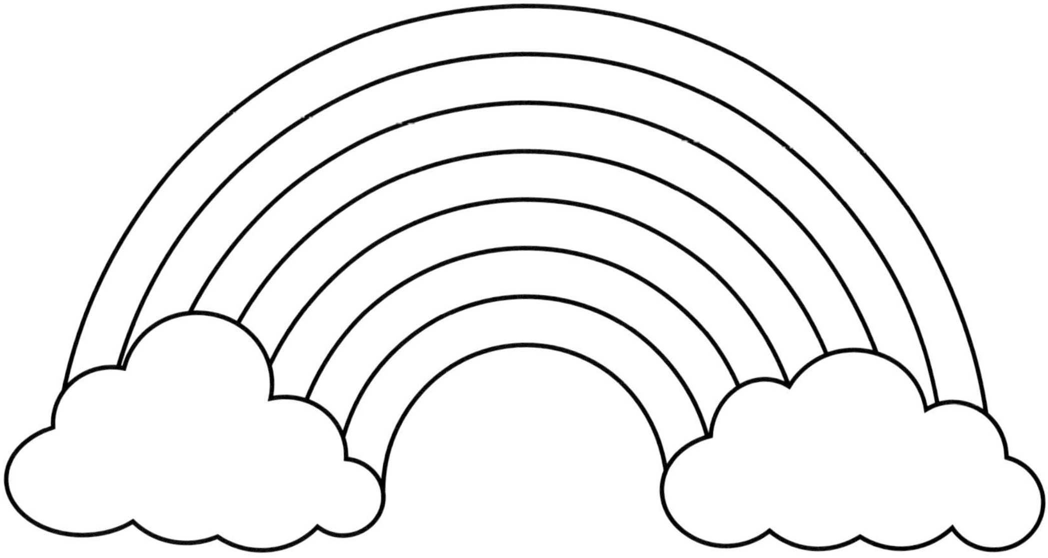

Which One?

I lost my instrument. Use the clues to figure out which instrument is mine.

> My instrument is not a drum.
>
> My instrument is black.
>
> My instrument has strings.

Answers on page 128.

Follow Me: page 6

Hidden Pattern: page 8

Find My Shadow: page 7

Memory: pages 9-10

Making Groups: page 11

Can fly?
2 (butterfly, ladybug)

Is yellow?
2 (butterfly, duckling)

Is a mammal?
4 (deer, gorilla, horse, squirrel)

Can breathe underwater?
1 (goldfish)

Find It: page 13

What Is It?: page 12

butterfly

pig

lizard

Secret Code: page 14

A L I O N can roar.

Which One?: page 15

butterfly

Match It: page 17

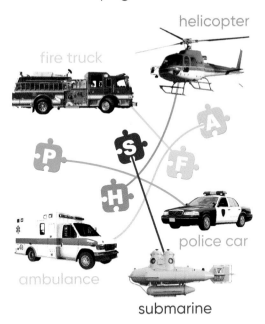

helicopter

fire truck

police car

ambulance

submarine

Follow Me: page 16

START

FINISH

Hidden Pattern: page 18

Zoom In: page 19

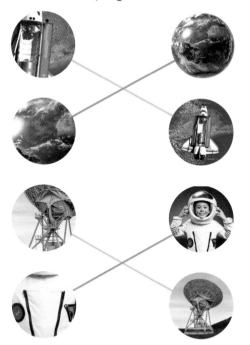

Two by Two: page 21

Hide and Seek: page 20

Step by Step: page 22

Making Groups: page 23

Is a fruit?
4 (apple, banana, pineapple, plum)

Is a vegetable?
3 (broccoli, carrot, corn)

Is baked?
3 (cake, cookies, cupcake)

Is a drink?
2 (milk, orange juice)

Find It: page 25

Missing Piece: page 24

Two by Two: page 26

What Is It?: page 27

mixer

snorkel

drum and drumsticks

Do It: pages 29-30

The robot's head fell off!

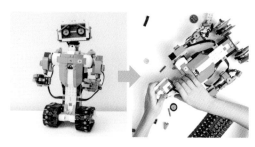

Follow Me: page 28

Find My Shadow: page 31

Draw It: page 32

Match It: page 34

guitar

drum

trumpet

piano

maracas

violin

T P V D G M

Secret Code: page 33

Let's bake B R E A D !

What Is Next?: page 35

 lemon

 plum

 blackberry

 orange

Hidden Pattern: page 36

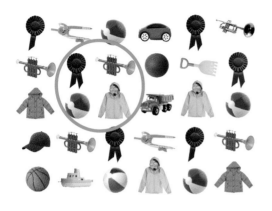

Zoom In: page 38

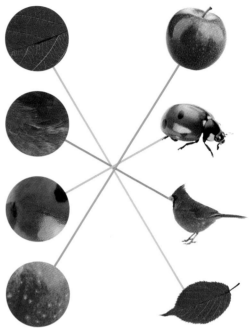

Step by Step: page 37

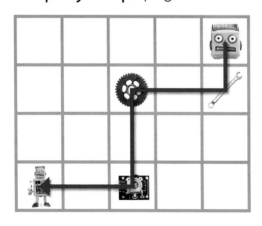

Memory: pages 39-40

Missing Piece: page 41

Which One?: page 43

flippers

Find My Shadow: page 42

Hide and Seek: page 44

Do It: pages 45–46

The watermelon got smashed!

Find It: page 48

Making Groups: page 47

Can fly?
3 (airplane, helicopter, spaceship)

Has wheels?
4 (airplane, bicycle, car, school bus)

Is red?
3 (bicycle, jet ski, spaceship)

Is yellow?
3 (excavator, school bus, submarine)

Match It: page 49

Secret Code: page 50

The V I O L I N

makes music.

Draw It: page 51

Follow Me: page 52

What Is Next?: page 53

 boat

 flip-flops

 rubber duck

 soccer ball

Answers

Hidden Pattern: page 54

Missing Piece: page 56

What Is It?: page 55

goldfish

koala

parakeet

Step by Step: page 57

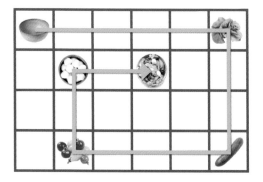

Zoom In: page 58

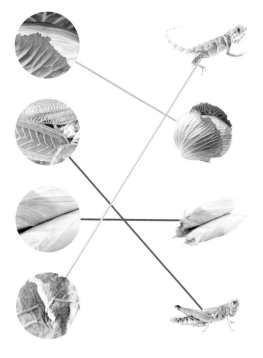

Find It: page 60

Out of Order: page 59

❸ SUMMER

❷ SPRING

❶ WINTER

❹ FALL

What Changed?: page 61

flipped ↵

What Is Next?: page 62

 butterfly

 dragonfly

 D

 H

 blue flower

 red flower

What Is It?: page 64

saxophone

brush

helmet

Find My Shadow: page 63

What Changed?: page 65

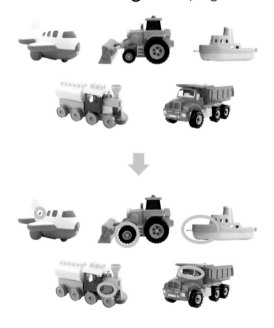

Two by Two: page 66

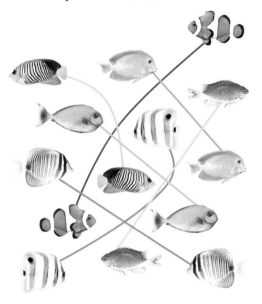

Hide and Seek: page 69

Do It: pages 67–68

The dog was brushed!

Which One?: page 70

orange

Match It: page 71

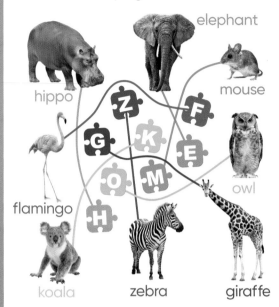

Hidden Pattern: page 73

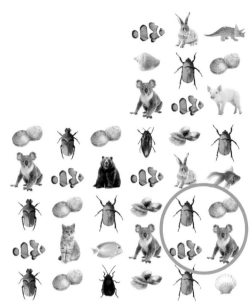

Secret Code: page 72

The B I C Y C L E goes fast.

Making Groups: page 74

Is blue?
2 (fish, crab)

Can swim?
7 (fish, crab, jellyfish, lobster, seal, turtle, blowfish)

Is not a mammal?
10 (blowfish, fish, clams, coral, crab, jellyfish, lobster, scallop, starfish, turtle)

Missing Piece: page 75

Zoom In: page 77

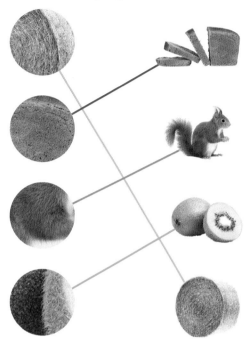

Two by Two: page 76

Draw It: page 78

Answers

What Is Next?: page 79

 rabbit

 cat

 S

 V

 beetroot

 mushroom

 onion

Find My Shadow: page 81

Follow Me: page 80

Out of Order: page 82

Step by Step: page 83

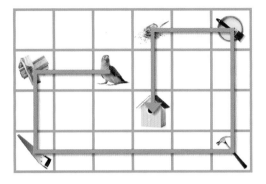

Which One?: page 85

soccer ball

Secret Code: page 84

The E L E P H A N T
is big.

Hidden Pattern: page 86

Memory: pages 87-88

Hide and Seek: page 90

Secret Code: page 89

The U M B R E L L A
is rainbow.

Two by Two: page 91

Match It: page 92

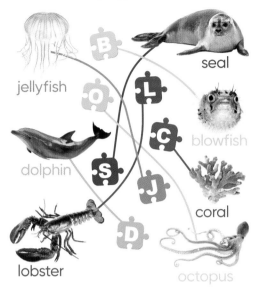

Draw It: page 94

Step by Step: page 93

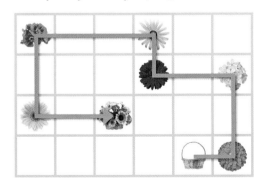

Out of Order: page 95

What Changed?: page 96

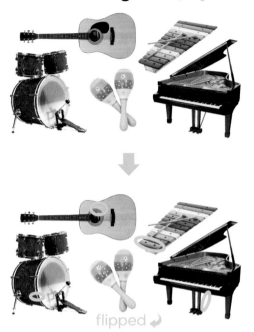

flipped

Follow Me: page 98

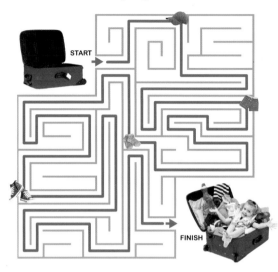

START

FINISH

Hide and Seek: page 97

Out of Order: page 99

What Changed?: page 100

flipped ↩

Missing Piece: page 102

Find It: page 101

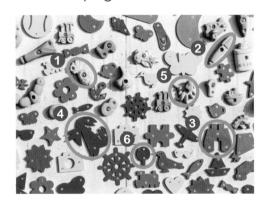

Out of Order: page 103

1. RED
2. ORANGE
3. YELLOW
4. GREEN
5. BLUE
6. INDIGO
7. VIOLET

Which One?: page 104

guitar